This journal belongs to

_____

Grounded in Gratitude
Journaling to Joy

Roxanne Glaser

Grounded in Gratitude: Journaling to Joy

ISBN: 9781097110469

First Edition 2019, Revised October 2021
SDG Design Publications
Waco, Texas, 76712

WITH MUCH GRATITUDE

Gratitude has helped me transform my journey through grief into one of hope and joy. May I thankful for many people and experiences along the way. Countless small, thoughtful gestures touched my heart.

This journal is dedicated to my yoga teachers, Jess and Kim, for their encouragement and guidance. May I truly grateful for their presence in my life and for bringing me back to my mat time and time again.

For Tracy who sent me the journal that changed my life and shifted my perspective from loss and grief to gratitude and possibility. She is an amazing light and courageous role model for others.

For Becky who guided me through the GriefShare process three times! She gave me tools to process the grief and a hope that I would smile and laugh again one day.

Contents

What is Gratitude?.. 1

Why Practice Gratitude? 1

How To Use This Journal 1

Example Page.. 3

Accountability Heart Chart 5

Gratitude Exercises and Activities........................... 77

Calming Breath 79

Gratitude Meditations 79

What is Doodle OM? 81

Why Doodle Spirals? 81

Doodle Om Practice 83

Favorite Gratitude Quotes....................................... 95

Books to Spark Gratitude... 95

WHAT IS GRATITUDE?

Gratitude is embracing your current situation and being thankful. A daily practice of gratitude is one of the key dimensions of joy.

WHY PRACTICE GRATITUDE?

A daily practice of gratitude provides many benefits, both mental and physical.

- Creates empathy.
- Shifts perspective.
- Increases serotonin levels.
- Increases dopamine levels.
- Increases endorphins.
- Enables thoughts to become actions.
- Improves sleep.
- Improves self-esteem. .

HOW TO USE THIS JOURNAL

This journal is a quick check-in for you in the morning and evening. Place it near your bed with a favorite pen. Write in it immediately in the morning when you wake up and make it the last thing you do before you fall asleep.

Keep in mind the following guidelines:

- Gratitude is expressing your thankfulness or what you are seeking to bring into your life.
- "Something great" should be within your control. As you write these items, I know it would be great if you won the lottery, but work to focus on actions and attitudes that are realistic, practical, and within your power.
- The affirmation is another key for setting the tone for your day. If you have the same affirmation or mantra each day, write it out every day. Eventually this becomes a belief in your mind which translates to actions. Then things start to happen.

Day __Monday__   Date _____/_____/_____

_____Teach yoga and go to softball_____

_____*NOTE:* This space is for anything you want to add._____

_____

May I grateful for

- _Seeing sunshine outside my window_
- _A great cup of coffee_
- _Friends to hike with_

How can I make today great?

- _Being present in conversations_
- _Getting to bed by 10:30_
- _Making time to create something_

May I _be calm and confident in my interactions._

_____

_____

These amazing things happened today!

- _I discovered a new pen that I love._
- _Didn't look at my phone any during Coffee Talk!_
- _Took a short walk outside after dinner._

What could I have done to make today better?

Continue to work on leaving the phone alone. Be mindful.

_____

_____

ACCOUNTABILITY HEART CHART

This page is for you to track your progress. You can color in each heart or write a word that summarizes the day. Use this for motivation and to visually see your progress through the journey.

I, _____, commit to a daily gratitude practice beginning on _____.

I promise to write in my journal DAILY for _____ days in a row.

Signed,

_____

Day_____   Date _____/_____/_____

_____

_____

_____

_____

May I grateful for

-   _____

-   _____

-   _____

How can I make today great?

-   _____

-   _____

-   _____

May I _____

_____

_____

These amazing things happened today!

-   _____

-   _____

-   _____

What could I have done to make today better?

_____

_____

_____

Day_____ Date ____/____/____

_____

_____

_____

_____

May I grateful for

- _____

- _____

- _____

How can I make today great?

- _____

- _____

- _____

May I _____

_____

_____

These amazing things happened today!

- _____

- _____

- _____

What could I have done to make today better?

_____

_____

_____

Day_____   Date _____/_____/_____

_____

_____

_____

_____

May I grateful for

- _____

- _____

- _____

How can I make today great?

- _____

- _____

- _____

May I _____

_____

_____

These amazing things happened today!

- _____

- _____

- _____

What could I have done to make today better?

_____

_____

_____

Day_____   Date _____/_____/_____

_____

_____

_____

_____

May I grateful for

- _____

- _____

- _____

How can I make today great?

- _____

- _____

- _____

May I _____

_____

_____

These amazing things happened today!

- _____

- _____

- _____

What could I have done to make today better?

_____

_____

_____

Day_____   Date _____/_____/_____

_____

_____

_____

_____

May I grateful for

- _____

- _____

- _____

How can I make today great?

- _____

- _____

- _____

May I _____

_____

_____

These amazing things happened today!

- _____

- _____

- _____

What could I have done to make today better?

_____

_____

_____

Day_____   Date _____/_____/_____

_____
_____
_____
_____

May I grateful for

- _____
- _____
- _____

How can I make today great?

- _____
- _____
- _____

May I _____
_____
_____

These amazing things happened today!

- _____
- _____
- _____

What could I have done to make today better?

_____
_____
_____

Day_____   Date ____/____/____

_____

_____

_____

_____

May I grateful for

-   _____
-   _____
-   _____

How can I make today great?

-   _____
-   _____
-   _____

May I _____

_____

_____

These amazing things happened today!

-   _____
-   _____
-   _____

What could I have done to make today better?

_____

_____

_____

Day_____   Date _____/_____/_____

_____

_____

_____

_____

May I grateful for

- • _____

- • _____

- • _____

How can I make today great?

- • _____

- • _____

- • _____

May I _____

_____

_____

These amazing things happened today!

- • _____

- • _____

- • _____

What could I have done to make today better?

_____

_____

_____

Day_____   Date _____/_____/_____

_____

_____

_____

_____

May I grateful for

- _____

- _____

- _____

How can I make today great?

- _____

- _____

- _____

May I _____

_____

_____

These amazing things happened today!

- _____

- _____

- _____

What could I have done to make today better?

_____

_____

_____

Day_____   Date _____/_____/_____

_____

_____

_____

_____

May I grateful for

- _____

- _____

- _____

How can I make today great?

- _____

- _____

- _____

May I _____

_____

_____

These amazing things happened today!

- _____

- _____

- _____

What could I have done to make today better?

_____

_____

_____

Day_____   Date _____/_____/_____

_____
_____
_____
_____

May I grateful for

- _____
- _____
- _____

How can I make today great?

- _____
- _____
- _____

May I _____

_____
_____

These amazing things happened today!

- _____
- _____
- _____

What could I have done to make today better?

_____
_____
_____

Day_____   Date _____/_____/_____

_____

_____

_____

_____

May I grateful for

- _____

- _____

- _____

How can I make today great?

- _____

- _____

- _____

May I _____

_____

_____

These amazing things happened today!

- _____

- _____

- _____

What could I have done to make today better?

_____

_____

_____

Day_____   Date _____/_____/_____

_____
_____
_____
_____

May I grateful for

- _____
- _____
- _____

How can I make today great?

- _____
- _____
- _____

May I _____
_____
_____

These amazing things happened today!

- _____
- _____
- _____

What could I have done to make today better?

_____
_____
_____

Day_____   Date _____/_____/_____

_____

_____

_____

_____

May I grateful for

- _____

- _____

- _____

How can I make today great?

- _____

- _____

- _____

May I _____

_____

_____

These amazing things happened today!

- _____

- _____

- _____

What could I have done to make today better?

_____

_____

_____

FIND
GOOD
IN THE
Situation
you are in

Day_____   Date _____/_____/_____

_____

_____

_____

_____

May I grateful for

- _____

- _____

- _____

How can I make today great?

- _____

- _____

- _____

May I _____

_____

_____

These amazing things happened today!

- _____

- _____

- _____

What could I have done to make today better?

_____

_____

_____

Day_____   Date _____/_____/_____

_____
_____
_____
_____

May I grateful for

- _____
- _____
- _____

How can I make today great?

- _____
- _____
- _____

May I _____
_____
_____

These amazing things happened today!

- _____
- _____
- _____

What could I have done to make today better?

_____
_____
_____

41

Day_____   Date _____/_____/_____

_____

_____

_____

_____

May I grateful for

- _____

- _____

- _____

How can I make today great?

- _____

- _____

- _____

May I _____

_____

_____

These amazing things happened today!

- _____

- _____

- _____

What could I have done to make today better?

_____

_____

_____

Day_____   Date _____/_____/_____

_____

_____

_____

_____

May I grateful for

- • _____

- • _____

- • _____

How can I make today great?

- • _____

- • _____

- • _____

May I _____

_____

_____

These amazing things happened today!

- • _____

- • _____

- • _____

What could I have done to make today better?

_____

_____

_____

Day_____   Date _____/_____/_____

_____

_____

_____

_____

May I grateful for

- • _____

- • _____

- • _____

How can I make today great?

- • _____

- • _____

- • _____

May I _____

_____

_____

These amazing things happened today!

- • _____

- • _____

- • _____

What could I have done to make today better?

_____

_____

_____

Day_____   Date _____/_____/_____

_____

_____

_____

_____

May I grateful for

- • _____

- • _____

- • _____

How can I make today great?

- • _____

- • _____

- • _____

May I _____

_____

_____

These amazing things happened today!

- • _____

- • _____

- • _____

What could I have done to make today better?

_____

_____

_____

Day_____   Date _____/_____/_____

_____

_____

_____

_____

May I grateful for

- •   _____

- •   _____

- •   _____

How can I make today great?

- •   _____

- •   _____

- •   _____

May I _____

_____

_____

These amazing things happened today!

- •   _____

- •   _____

- •   _____

What could I have done to make today better?

_____

_____

_____

Day_____   Date _____/_____/_____

_____

_____

_____

_____

May I grateful for

-   _____

-   _____

-   _____

How can I make today great?

-   _____

-   _____

-   _____

May I _____

_____

_____

These amazing things happened today!

-   _____

-   _____

-   _____

What could I have done to make today better?

_____

_____

_____

Day_____   Date _____/_____/_____

_____

_____

_____

_____

May I grateful for

- • _____

- • _____

- • _____

How can I make today great?

- • _____

- • _____

- • _____

May I _____

_____

_____

These amazing things happened today!

- • _____

- • _____

- • _____

What could I have done to make today better?

_____

_____

_____

Day_____   Date _____/_____/_____

_____

_____

_____

_____

May I grateful for

- _____

- _____

- _____

How can I make today great?

- _____

- _____

- _____

May I _____

_____

_____

These amazing things happened today!

- _____

- _____

- _____

What could I have done to make today better?

_____

_____

_____

Day_____   Date ____/____/____

_____

_____

_____

_____

May I grateful for

- _____

- _____

- _____

How can I make today great?

- _____

- _____

- _____

May I _____

_____

_____

These amazing things happened today!

- _____

- _____

- _____

What could I have done to make today better?

_____

_____

_____

Day_____   Date _____/_____/_____

_____

_____

_____

_____

May I grateful for

- •   _____

- •   _____

- •   _____

How can I make today great?

- •   _____

- •   _____

- •   _____

May I _____

_____

_____

These amazing things happened today!

- •   _____

- •   _____

- •   _____

What could I have done to make today better?

_____

_____

_____

Day_____   Date _____/_____/_____

_____

_____

_____

_____

May I grateful for

- _____

- _____

- _____

How can I make today great?

- _____

- _____

- _____

May I _____

_____

_____

These amazing things happened today!

- _____

- _____

- _____

What could I have done to make today better?

_____

_____

_____

65

Day_____   Date _____/_____/_____

_____

_____

_____

_____

May I grateful for

-   _____

-   _____

-   _____

How can I make today great?

-   _____

-   _____

-   _____

May I _____

_____

_____

These amazing things happened today!

-   _____

-   _____

-   _____

What could I have done to make today better?

_____

_____

_____

the Root of
JOY
is
gratefulness

Day_____   Date _____/_____/_____

_____
_____
_____
_____

May I grateful for

- •   _____
- •   _____
- •   _____

How can I make today great?

- •   _____
- •   _____
- •   _____

May I _____

_____
_____

These amazing things happened today!

- •   _____
- •   _____
- •   _____

What could I have done to make today better?

_____
_____
_____

Day_____   Date _____/_____/_____

_____

_____

_____

_____

May I grateful for

- _____

- _____

- _____

How can I make today great?

- _____

- _____

- _____

May I _____

_____

_____

These amazing things happened today!

- _____

- _____

- _____

What could I have done to make today better?

_____

_____

_____

Day_____   Date _____/_____/_____

_____

_____

_____

_____

May I grateful for

- _____

- _____

- _____

How can I make today great?

- _____

- _____

- _____

May I _____

_____

_____

These amazing things happened today!

- _____

- _____

- _____

What could I have done to make today better?

_____

_____

_____

GRATITUDE EXERCISES AND ACTIVITIES

Art Journaling: Use a variety of art supplies and relax your mind. As you settle into the flow of creating, begin to think of things for which you are grateful. Add words or pictures to the journal.

Doodle Om: Use this technique to focus your mind and allow thoughts to flow freely. Repeating a pattern allows the mind to focus and the subconscious thoughts to move to front of mind.

Gratitude Jar: Place a large jar with small slips of paper and a pen near it. Each morning write something you are thankful for on one of the slips of paper and place it in the jar. At the end of the year, empty the jar and read through them.

Physical Object: Find a physical object that brings a smile to your heart and keep it near. Whenever you touch it, think of three things that you are thankful for right at that moment.

Gratitude Walk: Take a stroll and set a certain number of things to think of that you are grateful for. Another idea is to go down the alphabet and think of a word that starts with that letter.

Gratitude Letter or Visit: Write a hand-written note to someone listing things that you are thankful for about them. Mail it to them or take it to them and read it aloud to them.

CALMING BREATH

1. Take a long, slow breath in through your nose. Filling your lower lungs first, then filling your upper lungs.
2. Pause. Relax your facial muscles. Relax your jaw. Relax your shoulders.
3. Slowly exhale through your nose.
4. Pause. Repeat

GRATITUDE MEDITATIONS

Grateful Mantra Meditation
- Sit quietly. Center yourself with breath.
- Breathe slowly and deeply.
- Repeat the following mantra 10 times.
  "I am grateful for _____."

Flip Perspective Gratitude Practice
- Sit quietly. Center yourself with breath.
- Think of something that is troubling you. Start small.
  i.e. The traffic today was horrible.
- Think of a way to shift or flip the perspective, looking for something positive.
  i.e. I got to listen to an extra episode of my favorite podcast on the way home.
- Continue to identify things that you are not happy with and try to find a positive.
- In any challenge, there is always a lesson.

WHAT IS DOODLE OM?

First, let's define doodling. Doodling is simply making marks on the page. There is no right or wrong way to doodle. You cannot doodle incorrectly. So, if you thought I was going to give you a drawing lesson and you were already saying, "I can't even draw a straight line," relax, no straight lines required.

The range of doodling is a spectrum from completely free form to highly structured. Some structured processes have specific patterns and size requirements.

Doodle Om is how we use doodling to quiet and still the mind. Select one pen and create a simple pattern. Repeat that pattern throughout the entire page.

The goal is not to create art or to judge the outcome. Remain non-attached to whatever you create. Simply focus on your breath and continue moving the pen. After you finish your Doodle Om session, sit quietly and look at what emerged on your page.

WHY DOODLE SPIRALS?

When you look at my artwork, you will notice that I use a lot of spirals. Did you know that some of the earliest spirals are believed to have been carved around 2500-3000 B.C.?

The spiral is a sacred symbol that represents the journey and change of life as it unfolds; taking a labyrinth-like passage that leads to the source. The spiral symbol can represent the consciousness of nature, beginning from its center, expanding outwardly.

DOODLE OM PRACTICE

Find a spot on the page. Begin with a dot. Slowly create a spiral around the dot, keeping your pen on the page. Let the lines be as near each other as you can get them without letting them touch. Breathe.

Gratitude turns what we have into enough.

Gratitude brings joy and laughter into your life.

Gratitude changes the energy you send into the world.

Gratitude creates abundance.

"One single grateful thought raised to heaven is
the most perfect prayer."

~Gotthold Lessing

FAVORITE GRATITUDE QUOTES

Between stimulus and response, there is a space. In that space lies your power to choose your response. In your response lies your growth and your freedom.
- *Viktor Frankl*

"Joy is a step beyond happiness. Happiness is a sort of atmosphere you can live in sometimes if you are lucky. Joy is a light that fills you with HOPE, FAITH, and LOVE.
~*Adela Rogers St. John*

Gratitude is a quality similar to electricity. It must be produced and discharged and used up in order to exist at all.
~*William Faulkner*

BOOKS TO SPARK GRATITUDE

A Beautiful Morning: How a Morning Ritual Can Feed Your Soul and Transform Your Life
> "Gratitude attracts more reasons to be grateful. When you start the day thinking about what's good in your life and feeling thankful for it, you clear the pathway for more good to come. Look for things to appreciate, and you will find more and more of them."
>
> Ashley Brown

Embrace Your Journey: A Coloring Book for Navigating Life
> "It is not what happens to us, but rather our reactions and our perspective that helps us learn, grow, and move through life."
>
> Roxanne Glaser

From Grief to Growth

"Finding joy during tough times is hard. The act of practicing gratitude and helping others creates space for healing."

Roxanne Glaser

Joyful: The Surprising Power of Ordinary Things to Create Extraordinary Happiness

"The power of the aesthetics of joy is that they speak directly to our unconscious minds, bringing out the best in us without our even being aware of it."

Ingrid Fetell Lee

The Gifts of Imperfection: Let Go of Who You Think You're Supposed to Be and Embrace Who You Are

"If we are not practicing gratitude and allowing ourselves to know joy; we are missing out on the two things that will actually sustain us during the inevitable hard times.

Brené Brown

The Book of Joy: Lasting Happiness in a Changing World
Dalai Lama, Desmond Tutu, and Douglas Abrams

"The three factors that seem to have the greatest influence on increasing our happiness are our ability to reframe our situation more positively, our ability to experience gratitude, and our choice to be kind and generous."

Dalai Lama

"Much depends on your attitude. If you are filled with negative judgment and anger, then you will feel separate from other people. You will feel lonely. But if you have an open heart and are filled with trust and friendship, even if you are physically alone, even living a hermit's life, you will never feel lonely."

Desmond Tutu

The Power of Now: A Spiritual Guide to Enlightenment
"There have been many people for whom limitation, failure, loss, illness, or pain in whatever form turned out to be their greatest teacher. It gave them depth, humility, and compassion. It made them more real."

Eckhart Tolle

ABOUT THE AUTHOR

Roxanne Glaser is a self-taught artist who sparks joy with her art and illustrations. She has always enjoyed the process of creating since she was a young girl. When her husband and sister passed away unexpectedly, she turned to art to help process the grief and begin rebuilding her life.

Inspired by nature and her personal yoga practice (plus LOTS of coffee with some kayaking), Roxanne's art touches hearts and minds with themes of transformation and encouragement. She shares her passion for creativity through workshops enabling others to reconnect with their authentic selves.

The designs and patterns in this book are for personal use only. Please contact us directly if you have interest in licensing Roxanne's work for use with your products or services.

You can find her work online at
www.superdoodlegirl.com.
Her books are available online at Amazon.